FROSTINGS

COURTNEY DIAL WHITMORE

PHOTOGRAPHS by
KYLE DREIER

GIBBS SMITH
TO ENRICH AND INSPIRE HUMANKIND

DEDICATION

To my boys; Chris for being my ultimate taste-tester, and Henry for sitting diligently by my side during this book's creation and not getting even one lick. The last recipe is for you, Henry.

ACKNOWLEDGMENTS

There are lots of special people who helped make the dream of a *Frostings* book come alive! A huge thank-you to Kyle Dreier and Caroline Brewer for turning my recipes into artwork. You're a dream team. Thank you to Tessa Huff for helping me put the "icing on the cake" and your excitement over this project. Thank you to Jill Rigsby for diligently taste-testing frostings for hours on end and being a mixing-bowl-washing queen. Thank you to my husband for allowing our house to look like a frosting war zone for several months. Thank you to my brother, David, for his assistance in helping me with the culinary details of many of these frostings. Thank you to Jennifer Baumann for giving a web presence to my books. Thank you also to Hilari Schaefer, Alison Oliver, Mollie Jannasch, Rory White, and Ian Riley for your roles in making this book a reality. Thank you to Hollie Keith, Suzanne Taylor, Dan Moench, Kim Eddy, and the Gibbs Smith team for another wonderful project.

As always, thank you to the enthusiastic readers of Pizzazzerie.com who continue to inspire me to create and entertain in style! You are the reason I get to do what I love every day.

TABLE of CONTENTS

INTRODUCTION

There are two kinds of people in this world. You're either a frosting person or a cake person. You can probably imagine which one I am. I was the little girl that ate the cake in my birthday cake slice first so that the delicious frosting was left last, and I could savor each bite of sugary sweetness. I'm still that little girl. It's obvious what type of person this book is for. I like to think that "frosting" people are the creative ones, the thrill-seekers, the ones that appreciate the art of a perfectly tied bow and perfectly decorated party, the ones that love the "icing on the cake!" This book is for you! Dig in . . .

A little history lesson . . .

The first "icings" were created in the mid-seventeenth century and consisted of boiled sugar, egg whites, and flavorings like rose water. It was a pourable icing that produced a thick, glossy covering over cakes. In the mid-nineteenth century, frostings as we know them were developed. *The Cassell's New Universal Cookery Book* (London, 1894) contained the first mention of cake made with flour and sugar rather than yeast. Shortly after that, buttercream recipes began replacing boiled sugar frostings.

Most American palettes prefer a buttercream frosting similar to what they grew up enjoying on birthday cakes. It's an easy frosting to decorate and cover cakes, cupcakes, and other treats. This book contains my favorite buttercream recipes as well as recipes for other types of frostings or "icings" such as glazes, ganaches, and boiled sugar frostings.

My hope is that you will discover your new favorite frosting but also enjoy experimenting with new flavor combinations. Frostings are similar to ice cream; you can flavor them and add mix-ins to enhance flavor and color. Many of these frosting flavor varieties were inspired by favorite ice cream flavors. I encourage you to mix and match your favorite flavors, colors, and candies to create your perfect frosting. As for mine? Well it is on page 35.

TIPS & TECHNIQUES

EQUIPMENT

- The fundamental piece of equipment for frostings is an electric mixer. You can use either a standing electric mixer (paddle and whisk attachments) or an electric hand-mixer.
- Candy thermometer
- Double broiler (a heat-safe bowl over a saucepan of water can be substituted)
- Pastry bags and piping tips
- Food coloring gel
- Flavorings and extracts
- Spatulas and scrapers
- Whisk

See resources in back for recommendations on where to buy the items above.

BUTTER & SHORTENING

Butter and shortening are often exchanged for each other in frosting recipes. Butter is roughly 80 percent fat while shortening is 100 percent fat. Shortening in a frosting will produce a fluffier frosting that easily holds its shape for piped decorations. Frosting made with butter will have a slight yellowish tint. You can use 50 percent butter and 50 percent shortening or other combinations of fats in your recipes.

For a richer flavor, I recommend using unsalted grade A butter at room temperature. Try to use the highest-quality butter possible when making frostings. It is best not to soften butter in the microwave as it will begin to melt. All recipes in this book should use room temperature butter unless otherwise noted. To bring butter to room temperature, set it on a counter for at least 25 minutes.

Unsalted butter is recommended because it allows you more control over flavor because you can add salt in small amounts to your frostings.

CHOCOLATE

Always use the highest-quality chocolate you can buy to provide a richer taste in your frostings. Use the chart below for assistance with types of chocolate. You can often find high-quality chocolate in the candy aisle in bar form. This can be chopped (or grated on top!) for use in these frosting recipes.

Unsweetened chocolate—100% cocoa
Bittersweet chocolate—65–80% cocoa
Semisweet chocolate—35–50% cocoa
Dark chocolate—Contains no milk, at least 35% cocoa
Milk chocolate—at least 12% milk, usually 33–45% cocoa
White chocolate—not actually chocolate, contains 0% cocoa but instead consists of sugar, milk, and 20% cacao butter

POWDERED SUGAR

Always sift your powdered sugar prior to use (especially in glazes!) to avoid clumps. Powdered sugar is also called confectioners' sugar.

EXTRACTS

Natural extracts are made with a variety of special oils and alcohol. You can find them in the grocery store (spice or baking aisle). They are used to enhance flavors of baked goods and, of course, frostings! You can find a variety of unusual flavor extracts online (see resources in back). It is best to start with a small amount of extracts (1/4 teaspoon) and increase by taste.

PIPING BAGS

You will find frosting decorating bags in three varieties: featherweight, disposable bags, and parchment triangles. Featherweight bags are reusable and made of coated polyester. Disposable bags are a clear triangular bag that comes in a variety of sizes. Parchment triangles are another common disposable bag for piping. For a makeshift piping bag, snip the corner of a plastic bag.

FROSTING TIPS

Thicker frosting recipes will produce a prettier piped decoration out of a frosting tip. You can always add more powdered sugar to a frosting to thicken it. A rule of thumb is that a knife sliced through the frosting should hold its indention shape for a frosting that is perfect for piping. If it molds back together, it is too loose for piping.

Large tips will produce a pretty cupcake decoration (large round tip, French tip, etc.). You will need large couplers to pair with your tips.

COLORING

Food coloring gels will produce a richer color without changing the consistency of your frosting. You can find a variety of gel colors at Michaels or other craft stores as well as specialty cake-decorating stores. Use a toothpick to drop the color into your frosting. Always remember to start slowly; it's much easier to add color than try to adjust a color you dislike.

STORAGE & USE

You can save frostings in airtight containers in the refrigerator for up to a week. To use, bring to room temperature on a counter rather than heating. You can beat frostings for a couple of minutes to bring frosting back to a fluffy texture. For outdoor events, be mindful of frostings and remove them from direct sunlight. Frostings left in direct sunlight will melt and not hold their pretty piped texture. I recommend Italian Meringue Buttercream made with pasteurized egg whites for longer outdoor events. It holds its shape better than other frostings but do be mindful of frostings in sunlight.

The recipes (unless otherwise noted) will produce enough frosting for 12 piped cupcakes (or 24 cupcakes with frosting spread on top instead of piped) or two 8-inch cakes. This is roughly $4^1/_2$ cups.

FROSTING CHEAT SHEET

1 tablespoon = 3 teaspoons
1 cup butter = 2 sticks
$^1/_2$ cup butter = 1 stick
1 pound sifted powdered sugar = $4^1/_2$ cups
1 pound unsifted powdered sugar = 4 cups
12 ounces chocolate chips = 2 cups

BUTTERCREAM FLAVORS

Get creative and add a variety of flavors to your frosting after butter is incorporated.

Chocolate—Add 6–8 ounces melted semi-sweet chocolate.
Almond—Add 2 teaspoons almond extract.
Raspberry—Add 2 tablespoons raspberry jam (or raspberry puree).
Orange—Add 1 tablespoon orange liqueur or orange extract and grated orange zest.
Coffee—Add 2 teaspoons instant espresso powder with 2 tablespoons warm water.
Your choice—Try out flavorings, extracts, jams, purees, and more to create your own unique flavor!

FROSTINGS

No, you're not about to get a geography lesson—just a frosting one! There are several types of buttercream frosting, including American, French, Swiss, and Italian. The basics of buttercream consist of creaming together fat (usually butter, hence the name) and sugar. They are easy to flavor and oh so delicious!

AMERICAN BUTTERCREAM

IN THE BOWL of an electric mixer fitted with the paddle attachment, beat butter for 2 minutes on medium speed. Adjust speed to low and add powdered sugar to butter 1 cup at a time until well incorporated. Add salt, vanilla extract, and milk or heavy cream. Beat on medium for 3 minutes. Add additional powdered sugar or milk/cream until desired consistency is reached. For firmer frosting, add more powdered sugar ($1/4$ cup at a time). For looser frosting, add more milk or cream (1 tablespoon at a time).

TIP: Classic buttercream, the frosting most of us know, is the American tradition. Made with butter and powdered sugar, it's the base for many of the recipes in this book as it is the easiest frosting to create.

MAKES 4$1/2$ CUPS

1 cup unsalted butter, softened
3-4 cups powdered sugar
$1/4$ teaspoon salt
1 tablespoon vanilla extract
3 tablespoons milk or heavy cream

FRENCH BUTTERCREAM

IN THE BOWL of an electric mixer fitted with the whisk attachment, beat egg yolks on high for 5 minutes until light and foamy. Add sugar and water into saucepan and bring to a boil while stirring. Continue to stir until sugar mixture reaches 240 degrees F. Immediately remove from heat and slowly pour sugar mixture down sides of mixer while on low. Increase speed to medium high and beat until mixture is room temperature and light in color (about 5–7 minutes). Cut softened butter in 1-inch cubes. Add in butter one cube at a time, allowing it to be incorporated as you go. Add vanilla extract and beat for 5 minutes on medium high. Refrigerate for 30 minutes before frosting.

TIP: French buttercream produces a rich buttery-tasting frosting that is silky, shiny, and very luxurious.

MAKES 4¹/₂ CUPS

3 ounces egg yolks (about 6 large eggs), room temperature
1 cup granulated sugar
¹/₄ cup water
1¹/₄ cups unsalted butter, softened
¹/₂ teaspoon vanilla extract

Swiss Meringue Buttercream

Fill a saucepan with about 1–2 inches of water and heat to a simmer. Add egg whites and sugar to your mixing bowl and place over saucepan. Whisk sugar mixture until temperature reaches 150 degrees F. Remove mixing bowl and beat with whisk attachment for 10 minutes on medium high (this is 8 on a Kitchen-Aid). The mixture will double in size, becoming thick and glossy. The mixing bowl should be cool on the bottom.

Add in butter one tablespoon at a time until fully incorporated. Add in vanilla extract and salt. Mix thoroughly until smooth and silky (this may take 5+ minutes).

Tip: The chosen buttercream for many cake decorators, Swiss meringue buttercream is light, fluffy, and satin-like in appearance.

Troubleshooting: If your frosting appears "curdled" or soupy at any point, don't worry! Just continue to beat for 3–4 minutes on medium high until a light and fluffy frosting appears.

Makes 4¹/₂ cups

- 5 large egg whites
- 1 cup plus 2 tablespoons granulated sugar
- 1 pound unsalted butter, cut into tablespoons, room temperature
- 1¹/₂ tablespoons pure vanilla extract (use clear for a pure white frosting)
- ¹/₄ teaspoon salt

Italian Meringue Buttercream

PLACE EGG WHITES in the bowl of an electric mixer fitted with the whisk attachment. Whip eggs on medium speed until frothy. Add cream of tartar and beat until soft peaks form. With mixer on low, pour in ¼ cup of sugar. Beat for another 1-2 minutes. In a saucepan over medium heat, combine water and remaining sugar (1 cup). Bring to a boil and cook to 238 degrees F. (or softball stage).

Carefully remove sugar syrup from heat and with mixer on low speed, gently pour the syrup down the side of the bowl while beating (with paddle attachment). Beat for 4-6 minutes or until bottom of bowl is no longer warm. Add butter, cut into tablespoons, piece by piece, until fully incorporated. Beat for 3-4 minutes until thick and fluffy.

TIP: One of my favorite frostings, Italian Meringue Buttercream, is smooth and buttery. It produces a gorgeous frosting for cakes!

TROUBLESHOOTING: If your frosting appears "curdled" or soupy at any point, don't worry! Just continue to beat for 3-4 minutes on medium high until a light and fluffy frosting appears.

MAKES 4½ CUPS

1 cup egg whites (about 5-6 egg whites)
¼ teaspoon cream of tartar
1¼ cups granulated sugar
½ cup water
1 pound unsalted butter, room temperature

COOKED FLOUR

WHISK TOGETHER FLOUR and milk in a saucepan over medium heat. Mixture will begin to thicken. Continue to stir together with whisk until it becomes thick, similar to brownie batter. Use the back of a spatula to remove any flour lumps. It will take the shape of a ball when rolled together. Remove from heat and let cool *completely* to room temperature. You can place flour mixture in refrigerator to speed up this process.

In the bowl of an electric mixer fitted with the whisk attachment, cream together butter and granulated sugar until creamy (about 2–3 minutes). Add cooled flour mixture and vanilla extract to creamed butter. Beat on medium high until light and fluffy (5–10 minutes).

TIP: Often called heritage frosting, this recipe uses cooked flour. It produces a very light and fluffy frosting that is not too sweet.

MAKES 4½ CUPS

5 tablespoons flour
1 cup milk
1 cup unsalted butter, room temperature
1 cup granulated sugar
2 teaspoons vanilla extract

WHIPPED GROCERY

COMBINE SHORTENING AND BUTTER in an electric mixer fitted with the paddle attachment. Once creamy, add powdered sugar 1 cup at a time until well incorporated. Mix in vanilla and water. Beat for 5-6 minutes until light and fluffy.

TIP: Most grocery store bakeries use a light, whipped frosting on their birthday cakes. This recipe emulates that sweet, fluffy frosting. It's a great one for kids' birthday cakes or anyone with a big sweet tooth. It's made with shortening so it produces a pure white frosting that holds its shape well when piped.

MAKES 4¹/₂ CUPS

1 cup shortening
¹/₂ cup butter
6 cups powdered sugar
1¹/₂ tablespoons vanilla
4 tablespoons water

RICH CHOCOLATE

IN THE BOWL of an electric mixer fitted with the paddle attachment, beat butter for 2 minutes on medium speed. Adjust speed to low and add powdered sugar to butter 1 cup at a time until well incorporated. Add salt, vanilla extract, and heavy cream or milk. Melt chocolate in a double boiler or carefully in a microwave. Pour melted chocolate into frosting. Beat on medium for 3 minutes. Add additional powdered sugar or milk/cream until desired consistency is reached. For firmer frosting, add more powdered sugar ($^1/_4$ cup at a time). For looser frosting, add more milk or cream (1 tablespoon at a time).

TIP: Prefer milk or dark chocolate? Trade out bittersweet for the chocolate of your choosing!

MAKES 4$^1/_2$ CUPS

1	cup unsalted butter
4	cups powdered sugar
$^1/_4$	cup dark cocoa powder
$^1/_8$	teaspoon salt
1	teaspoon vanilla extract
3	tablespoons heavy cream or milk
10	ounces bittersweet chocolate, chopped (70 percent cocoa or higher)

🌼 GARNISH IT!

Chocolate shavings

Sprinkles

Berries

CREAM CHEESE

IN THE BOWL of an electric mixer fitted with the paddle attachment, beat cream cheese and butter for 2 minutes on medium speed. Adjust speed to low and add powdered sugar to butter 1 cup at a time until well incorporated. Add vanilla extract, salt, and heavy cream or milk. Beat on medium for 3 minutes. Add additional powdered sugar or cream/milk until desired consistency is reached. For firmer frosting, add more powdered sugar (¼ cup at a time). For looser frosting, add more cream or milk (1 tablespoon at a time).

MAKES 4½ CUPS

8 ounces cream cheese, softened
½ cup unsalted butter
3½ cups powdered sugar
1 teaspoon vanilla extract
⅛ teaspoon salt
1–2 tablespoons heavy cream or milk

salted caramel

In a saucepan over medium heat, melt butter completely. Add brown sugar and cream. Stir until brown sugar is dissolved. Add in salt and bring to a boil for 1 minute. Allow to cool and come to room temperature. Place butter mixture in bowl of electric mixer fitted with paddle attachment. Add powdered sugar 1 cup at a time. Add additional salt to taste. Add additional powdered sugar to thicken frosting or heavy cream to loosen frosting.

$1/2$ cup unsalted butter

1 cup dark brown sugar

$1/3$ cup heavy cream

$1/2$ teaspoon kosher salt plus more for tasting

3 cups powdered sugar

Makes 4^1/$_2$ cups

 **GARNISH IT!**

Salted caramel drizzle

Sea salt

PUMPKIN SPICE

IN THE BOWL of an electric mixer fitted with the paddle attachment, beat butter for 2 minutes on medium speed. Add in canned pumpkin and beat for 1 minute. Adjust speed to low and add powdered sugar 1 cup at a time until well incorporated. Add salt, vanilla extract, spices, and milk or heavy cream. Add additional powdered sugar or milk until desired consistency is reached.

MAKES 4¹/₂ CUPS

¹/₄ cup unsalted butter
¹/₄ cup canned pure pumpkin
3¹/₂ cups powdered sugar
¹/₂ teaspoon salt
1 teaspoon vanilla extract
1 teaspoon cinnamon
¹/₄ teaspoon ground nutmeg
¹/₄ teaspoon ground cloves
1-2 tablespoons milk or heavy cream

 GARNISH IT!

Add a dash of pumpkin pie spice over the frosting

Gingerbread Cinnamon

In the bowl of an electric mixer fitted with the paddle attachment, beat butter for 2 minutes on medium speed. Adjust speed to low and add powdered sugar to butter 1 cup at a time until well incorporated. Add cinnamon, ginger, nutmeg, cloves, and heavy cream or milk. Beat on medium for 3 minutes.

Makes 4½ cups

- 1 cup unsalted butter
- 3 cups powdered sugar
- 1 tablespoon ground cinnamon
- 1 tablespoon ground ginger
- ¼ teaspoon ground nutmeg
- ¼ teaspoon ground cloves
- 1 tablespoon heavy cream or milk

 **GARNISH IT!**

Gingerbread cookies

Ground gingerbread crumbs

Cinnamon

SIMPLY ALMOND

IN THE BOWL of an electric mixer fitted with the paddle attachment, beat butter for 2 minutes on medium speed. Adjust speed to low and add powdered sugar to butter 1 cup at a time until well incorporated. Add almond extract and heavy cream. Beat on medium for 3 minutes. Add more powdered sugar to thicken frosting or milk to loosen frosting.

MAKES 4¹/₂ CUPS

1 cup unsalted butter
3-4 cups powdered sugar
1 tablespoon almond extract
2 tablespoons heavy cream

🌼 GARNISH IT!

Toasted almonds

Bananas Foster

Mash banana in a small bowl with lemon juice. In the bowl of an electric mixer fitted with the paddle attachment, cream butter until light and fluffy (about 1-2 minutes). Add mashed banana and beat for another 1-2 minutes until well mixed. Add powdered sugar 1 cup at a time. Add in brown sugar, cinnamon, rum (optional), and vanilla extract. Beat for 2 minutes. Add more powdered sugar to thicken frosting or milk to loosen frosting.

Tip: Bananas Foster is my favorite dessert so I had to turn this classic favorite into a frosting! It pairs well with all types of cakes, whoopee pies, even cookies! You can omit the rum or use rum extract. Want more banana flavor? Add in a teaspoon of banana extract.

Makes 4½ cups

- ½ cup banana, mashed (about 1 large banana)
- 1 teaspoon lemon juice
- 1 cup unsalted butter
- 4 cups powdered sugar
- 2 tablespoons dark brown sugar
- 1 tablespoon cinnamon
- 2 teaspoons dark rum (optional)
- 1 teaspoon vanilla extract

 GARNISH IT!

Sliced bananas

Sprinkled cinnamon

STRAWBERRY SUPREME

Puree strawberries in a food processor for 15 seconds or until fully pureed. Move to saucepan over medium heat and bring to a boil. Reduce to medium-low heat and stir often. Puree will reduce and darken in color.

In the bowl of an electric mixer fitted with the paddle attachment, beat butter for 2 minutes on medium speed. Adjust speed to low and add one cup of powdered sugar to butter. Alternate adding strawberry puree and powdered sugar until completely mixed. Add in salt, lemon juice, and vanilla extract and beat on medium for 1–2 minutes. To loosen, add milk. To thicken, add powdered sugar.

Makes 4½ cups

1 cup strawberries
1 cup unsalted butter
4 cups powdered sugar
¼ teaspoon salt
1 teaspoon lemon juice
1 teaspoon vanilla extract

❀ GARNISH IT!

Sliced strawberries

BROWNED BUTTER

PLACE BUTTER in a small saucepan over medium heat. Cook until butter turns slightly brown (small brown specks will appear on bottom of saucepan). Stir continuously. Be careful not to overcook (if you see black specks, you have overcooked). Remove from heat, cover, and allow to cool until solidified (you can place in a refrigerator for 20–25 minutes to speed up this process).

In the bowl of an electric mixer fitted with the paddle attachment, beat butter for 2 minutes on medium speed. Adjust speed to low and add powdered sugar to butter 1 cup at a time until well incorporated. Add vanilla extract, and milk or heavy cream. Beat on medium for 3 minutes. Add more powdered sugar to thicken frosting or milk/cream to loosen frosting.

TIP: Browned butter has a strong, nutty flavor that many people love! It's perfect for a fall-themed dessert.

MAKES 4$\frac{1}{2}$ CUPS

1 cup unsalted butter
3–4 cups powdered sugar
1$\frac{1}{2}$ teaspoons vanilla extract
$\frac{1}{4}$ cup milk or heavy cream

PEANUT BUTTER CUP LOVER'S

In THE BOWL of an electric mixer fitted with the paddle attachment, beat butter for 2 minutes on medium speed. Adjust speed to low and add powdered sugar to butter 1 cup at a time until well incorporated. Add vanilla extract, and milk or heavy cream, and peanut butter. Beat on medium for 3 minutes. Add additional powdered sugar or milk/cream until desired consistency is reached. Stir in chocolate chunks.

MAKES 4¹/₂ CUPS

¹/₂ cup unsalted butter
3 cups powdered sugar
¹/₂ teaspoon vanilla extract
3 tablespoons milk or heavy cream
1 cup peanut butter
¹/₂ cup chocolate chunks

 GARNISH IT!

Mini Reese's Peanut Butter Cups

Reese's Pieces

Chopped peanuts

Chocolate sundae topping

Kahlua

IN THE BOWL of an electric mixer fitted with the paddle attachment, beat butter for 2 minutes on medium speed. Add Kahlua and vanilla extract and beat for additional minute. Adjust speed to low and add powdered sugar to butter 1 cup at a time until well incorporated. Add more powdered sugar to thicken frosting or milk/cream to loosen frosting.

MAKES 4¹/₂ CUPS

1	cup unsalted butter
¹/₃	cup Kahlua
¹/₂	teaspoon vanilla extract
5	cups powdered sugar

 GARNISH IT!

Chocolate-covered espresso beans

Chocolate shavings

Chocolate sundae syrup

CHAI VANILLA BEAN

PLACE BUTTER and loose tea in a saucepan over medium heat. Once butter is melted, reduce to low heat and continue heating for 5 minutes. Remove from heat and allow to cool for 5 minutes. Pour butter mixture into sieve to remove tea leaves. Some butter will remain with tea pieces, which is fine. Let strained butter come to room temperature (or refrigerate for 20–25 minutes).

Cream butter in the bowl of an electric mixer fitted with the paddle attachment until light and fluffy (1–2 minutes). Add powdered sugar 1 cup at a time until thoroughly incorporated. Add in heavy cream, vanilla extract, and vanilla bean. Beat for 2–3 minutes. Add additional powdered sugar to thicken frosting or more cream to loosen.

MAKES 4$^1/_2$ CUPS

$1^1/_2$ cups unsalted butter
3 tablespoons loose chai tea (roughly 8 tea bags)
$3^1/_2$ cups powdered sugar
2–3 tablespoons heavy cream
1 teaspoon vanilla extract
1 vanilla bean, scraped

TOFFEE SUNDAE

CREAM BUTTER in the bowl of an electric mixer fitted with the paddle attachment until light and fluffy (1–2 minutes). Add powdered sugar 1 cup at a time until thoroughly incorporated. Add in heavy cream or milk, caramel sauce, and salt. Beat for 2–3 minutes. Add additional powdered sugar to thicken frosting or more cream/milk to loosen.

In a saucepan over medium heat, melt chocolate, butter, and oil until smooth. Remove from heat and drizzle over toffee frosting.

MAKES 4 1/2 CUPS

1 cup unsalted butter
4 cups powdered sugar
1 tablespoon heavy cream or milk
1/3 cup caramel sauce
1/8 teaspoon kosher salt

CHOCOLATE SUNDAE TOPPING

1 cup semi-sweet chocolate chips
1/4 cup unsalted butter
1/4 cup vegetable oil

🌼 GARNISH IT!

Heath Toffee Bits

Chocolate syrup

Cherry on top

COOKIES 'N' CREAM

IN THE BOWL of an electric mixer fitted with the paddle attachment, cream butter for 1 minute on medium speed. Add in marshmallow fluff and beat for another minute. Adjust speed to low and add powdered sugar to butter mixture 1 cup at a time until well incorporated. Add vanilla extract and milk. Beat on medium speed for 2–3 minutes. Add additional powdered sugar or milk/cream until desired consistency is reached. Stir in crushed Oreo cookies.

MAKES 4¹/₂ CUPS

1	cup unsalted butter
1	(7-ounce) container marshmallow fluff
3–4	cups powdered sugar
1	teaspoon vanilla extract
1	tablespoon milk
10	Oreo cookies, crushed

🌼 GARNISH IT!

Oreo cookies

CHOCOLATE CHIP COOKIE DOUGH

START BY MAKING cookie dough. In the bowl of an electric mixer fitted with the paddle attachment, cream together butter and brown sugar. Add in milk and vanilla extract. Add in flour and salt. Mix well. Stir in chocolate chips. Transfer to separate bowl.

In the electric mixer bowl, beat butter for 2 minutes on medium speed. Adjust speed to low and add powdered sugar to butter 1 cup at a time until well incorporated. Add salt, vanilla extract, and milk. Beat well and add in cookie dough mixture. Stir until incorporated.

MAKES 4 1/2 CUPS

 **GARNISH IT!**

Mini chocolate chips

Chocolate chip cookies

COOKIE DOUGH

- 1/2 cup butter, softened
- 2/3 cup dark brown sugar
- 2 teaspoons milk
- 1 teaspoon vanilla extract
- 1/2 cup flour
- 1/4 teaspoon salt
- 1/2 cup mini chocolate chips

FROSTING

- 1/2 cup unsalted butter, softened
- 2 cups powdered sugar
- 1/4 teaspoon salt
- 1/2 teaspoon vanilla extract
- 1 tablespoon milk

Key Lime Pie

IN THE BOWL of an electric mixer fitted with the paddle attachment, cream together butter and cream cheese until light and fluffy (1–2 minutes). Add powdered sugar 1 cup at a time. Add in key lime juice, zest, and salt. Beat for 1–2 minutes. Add more powdered sugar to thicken frosting or cream to loosen frosting.

MAKES 4^1/$_2$ CUPS

^{1}/$_2$ cup unsalted butter

8 ounces cream cheese, softened

3^1/$_2$–4 cups powdered sugar

3 tablespoons key lime juice

2 tablespoons grated lime zest

^{1}/$_8$ teaspoon kosher salt

 **GARNISH IT!**

Sliced lime and lime zest

Graham cracker crumbs

Whipped cream

Key lime cooler cookies

MINT CHOCOLATE CHIP

IN THE BOWL of an electric mixer fitted with the paddle attachment, beat butter for 2 minutes on medium speed. Adjust speed to low and add powdered sugar to butter 1 cup at a time until well incorporated. Add salt, vanilla extract, and milk or heavy cream. Add peppermint extract and food coloring. Beat on medium for 3 minutes. Add additional powdered sugar or milk/cream until desired consistency is reached. For firmer frosting, add more powdered sugar ($^1/_4$ cup at a time). For looser frosting, add more milk or cream (1 tablespoon at a time). Stir in mini chocolate chips.

MAKES 4$^1/_2$ CUPS

1 cup unsalted butter

3-4 cups powdered sugar

$^1/_4$ teaspoon kosher salt

1 tablespoon vanilla extract

3 tablespoons milk or heavy cream

$^1/_4$ teaspoon peppermint extract

5 drops green food coloring

$^2/_3$ cup mini chocolate chips

 **GARNISH IT!**

Mini chocolate chips

Chocolate chunks

CHAMPAGNE BUTTERCREAM

IN THE BOWL of an electric mixer fitted with the paddle attachment, beat butter for 2 minutes on medium speed. Adjust speed to low and add powdered sugar to butter 1 cup at a time until well incorporated. Add vanilla extract and Champagne. Beat on medium for 3 minutes. Add more powdered sugar to thicken frosting or milk to loosen frosting.

MAKES 4 1/2 CUPS

1 cup unsalted butter, room temperature
4 cups (1 pound) powdered sugar
1 teaspoon vanilla extract
3 tablespoons Champagne

 GARNISH IT!

Gold sprinkles

Gold luster dust

S'MORES

BEAT SOFTENED BUTTER and marshmallow fluff together in the bowl of an electric mixer fitted with the paddle attachment until smooth (1–2 minutes). Add extracts and milk and mix well. Slowly blend in powdered sugar and beat until smooth and creamy. To thin frosting, add more milk. To thicken frosting, add more powdered sugar.

MAKES 3 CUPS

1$\frac{1}{3}$ cups unsalted butter, room temperature

2 cups (7-ounce container) marshmallow fluff

$\frac{1}{2}$ tablespoon vanilla extract

$\frac{1}{2}$ tablespoon almond extract

1$\frac{1}{2}$ teaspoons milk

4–5 cups powdered sugar

 GARNISH IT!

Graham cracker crumbs

Mini marshmallows

Chocolate sundae sauce

Spiced Cookie

In the bowl of an electric mixer fitted with the paddle attachment, beat butter for 2 minutes on medium speed. Adjust speed to low and add powdered sugar to butter 1 cup at a time until well incorporated. Add vanilla extract, heavy cream, and Biscoff spread. Beat for 2 minutes. Stir in cookie crumbles.

Makes 4¹/₂ cups

¹/₂	cup unsalted butter, room temperature
3–4	cups powdered sugar
2	teaspoons vanilla extract
2	tablespoons heavy cream
1	cup Biscoff Spread
¹/₂	cup Biscoff cookies, crumbled (optional)

 **GARNISH IT!**

Cookie crumbles

Ganaches

Ganaches are decadent glazes and fillings in cakes traditionally made from heating cream and pouring over chocolate. You can drizzle ganache over desserts as a glaze or whip it for a fluffy texture. You can also allow it to cool into a truffle-like consistency for pretty, piped details. Typically, one part cream to two parts chocolate is used and enhanced with flavors or liqueurs.

MILK CHOCOLATE

PLACE THE CHOPPED CHOCOLATE in a medium heat-proof bowl. Heat the heavy cream in a medium saucepan over medium heat. Bring to a boil and remove from heat. Gently pour cream over chopped chocolate. Let bowl sit for 2 minutes. Using a whisk, mix together the cream and chocolate. Add butter and continue stirring. Use as a glaze or set aside to cool to room temperature. You can refrigerate to speed up the cooling process. Stir every 10 minutes or so until chilled and spreadable. You can also whip ganache and pipe it onto desserts.

MAKES 4¹/₂ CUPS

1 pound (16 ounces) milk chocolate, chopped

2 cups heavy cream

1 tablespoon unsalted butter

YUM
YUM
YUM

YUM
YUM
YUM

DARK CHOCOLATE

PLACE THE CHOPPED CHOCOLATE in a medium heat-proof bowl. Heat the heavy cream in a medium saucepan over medium heat. Bring to a boil and remove from heat. Gently pour cream over chopped chocolate. Let bowl sit for 2 minutes. Using a whisk, mix together the cream and chocolate. Add butter and liquor and continue stirring. Set aside to cool to room temperature. You can refrigerate to speed up the cooling process. Stir every 10 minutes or so until chilled and spreadable.

MAKES 4¹/₂ CUPS

1 pound (16 ounces) bittersweet chocolate, chopped

2 cups heavy cream

1 tablespoon unsalted butter

1 tablespoon cognac or brandy (optional)

WHITE CHOCOLATE

PLACE THE CHOPPED CHOCOLATE in a medium heat-proof bowl. Heat the heavy cream in a medium saucepan over medium heat. Bring to a boil and remove from heat. Gently pour cream over chopped chocolate. Let bowl sit for 2 minutes. Using a whisk, mix together the cream and chocolate. Add butter and continue stirring. Set aside to cool to room temperature. You can refrigerate to speed up the cooling process. Stir every 10 minutes or so until chilled and spreadable.

TIP: High-quality white chocolate will help ensure that your ganache thickens as it should.

MAKES 4¹/₂ CUPS

1 pound (16 ounces) white chocolate, chopped (high-quality white chocolate is important)
1¹/₂ cups heavy cream
1 tablespoon unsalted butter

MOCHA HAZELNUT

PLACE CHOPPED CHOCOLATE in a medium heat-proof bowl. Heat the heavy cream in a medium saucepan over medium heat. Bring to a boil and remove from heat. Gently pour cream over the chopped chocolate. Let bowl sit for 2 minutes. Using a whisk, mix together the cream and chocolate. Add butter, espresso, and hazelnut extract and continue stirring. You can use it as a glaze immediately or let it cool and then whip it into a frosting. You can refrigerate to speed up the cooling process. Stir every 10 minutes or so until chilled and spreadable.

MAKES 4¹/₂ CUPS

1 pound (16 ounces) bittersweet chocolate, chopped

2 cups heavy cream

1 tablespoon unsalted butter

2 teaspoons instant espresso powder

1 teaspoon hazelnut extract

CHERRY RUM

DRAIN CHERRIES and roughly chop. Stir in rum and set aside. Place chopped chocolate in a medium heat-proof bowl. Bring heavy cream to a boil and remove from heat. Pour cream over chopped chocolate. Stir together and add in cherries and rum. Stir gently until well mixed. You can use it as a glaze immediately or allowed to cool and then spread it between layers of cake.

MAKES 4¹/₂ CUPS

2 cups tart cherries, drained

3 tablespoons rum

12 ounces bittersweet chocolate, chopped

1 cup heavy cream

CHOCOLATE COCONUT

In a saucepan over medium heat, bring coconut milk almost to a boil. Remove and pour over chopped chocolate. Let sit for 1 minute and then whisk together until thoroughly mixed. You can use it as a glaze immediately or let it cool and then whip into a frosting.

MAKES 4¹/₂ CUPS

1¹/₂ cups coconut milk (full fat)

8 ounces bittersweet chocolate, chopped

8 ounces semi-sweet chocolate, chopped

GLAZES

I absolutely love glazes because they are the easiest to use. You simply dunk your treat in or pour it right over your cupcake, doughnut, bread, etc. Once you get the hang of it, you'll realize that glazes are super easy to make. I encourage you to get creative in the kitchen and whip up your own flavored glazes to add that perfect topping to your favorite dessert.

PETIT FOUR

Sift powdered sugar into a mixing bowl. Add in hot water and light corn syrup and extracts. Stir well until fully incorporated. Over a double boiler, melt white chocolate chips and vegetable oil. When melted, pour in sifted sugar mixture and stir until incorporated. Glaze is easier to pour when warm so continue to keep over heat (around 100–110 degrees F.).

Makes 1 ½ cups

2 cups powdered sugar

4 tablespoons hot water

3 tablespoons light corn syrup

½ cup white chocolate chips

1 tablespoon vegetable oil

1 teaspoon vanilla extract (clear)

1 teaspoon almond extract

RiCH CHOCOLaTe

In a microwave-safe bowl, combine butter, cream, light corn syrup, and vanilla extract. Microwave for 1 minute or until butter is melted. Stir in chopped chocolate until completely melted. Whisk in powdered sugar, ½ cup at a time.

MAKES 1 CUP

¼ cup unsalted butter

2 tablespoons heavy cream

½ tablespoon light corn syrup

½ teaspoon vanilla extract

2½ ounces bittersweet chocolate, chopped (70 percent cocoa)

1 cup powdered sugar

Vanilla Crème

In a medium bowl, whisk together powdered sugar, milk, extract, and cream cheese. Pour over desserts.

Makes 2 cups

1 cup powdered sugar

2 tablespoons milk

$1/4$ teaspoon vanilla extract

3 tablespoons cream cheese, softened

vaNilla BeaN

IN A MEDIUM BOWL, whisk together powdered sugar, milk, and extract. Split open vanilla bean and carefully scrape out vanilla beans. Stir into glaze.

MAKES 1 CUP

1 cup powdered sugar

2 tablespoons milk

1/4 tablespoon vanilla extract

1 vanilla bean

ZESTY LEMON

IN A MEDIUM BOWL, whisk together powdered sugar and lemon juice.

MAKES ½ CUP

1 cup powdered sugar

4 tablespoons lemon juice

PEANUT BUTTER

SIFT POWDERED SUGAR. Melt peanut butter in a microwave-safe bowl for 15–20 seconds or until warm. In a mixing bowl, whisk together powdered sugar, peanut butter, vanilla extract, and milk. Whisk until smooth. To make it easier to pour over desserts, heat glaze until warm.

MAKES 1 CUP

1½ cups powdered sugar
⅓ cup peanut butter
½ teaspoon vanilla extract
⅓ cup milk

BLueBeRRy

PULSE BLUEBERRIES in a food processor for about 15 seconds. Remove and run through sieve to remove seeds and skin. This should leave roughly $^3/_4$ cup blueberry juice (it will be a thick juice). Sift powdered sugar into mixing bowl. Add blueberry juice, softened butter, lemon juice, and vanilla extract. Whisk together until mixed.

MAKES 1 CUP

2 cups blueberries
1 cup powdered sugar
2 tablespoons butter, softened
1 teaspoon lemon juice
1 teaspoon vanilla extract

PUPCAKE FROSTING

BEAT CREAM CHEESE, peanut butter, oil, and honey together until mixed. Pipe your favorite dog treats or "pupcakes."

TIP: Henry, my English Springer Spaniel, sat by my side diligently during the creation of this book. The smells of chocolate, candy, and cookies wafted by his side but he wasn't allowed even one lick. This recipe is for him. It's for all the puppy lovers (perfect for puppy "pawties").

MAKES 4¹/₂ CUPS

8 ounces cream cheese, softened
¹/₂ cup peanut butter
2 tablespoons canola oil
1 teaspoon honey

Resources

EQUIPMENT
Electric Mixers
Kitchen-Aid: kitchenaid.com
Cuisinart: cuisinart.com

Piping Bags, Tips, Food Coloring Gel
Ateco Products
Wilton: wilton.com

FLAVORINGS & EXTRACTS
McCormick: mccormick.com
Nielsen-Massey: nielsenmassey.com
Sonoma Syrup: sonomasyrup.com

CAKE STANDS
Fishs Eddy: fishseddy.com
Home Goods: homegoods.com
Mosser Glass: www.mosserglass.com
Rosanna, Inc.: rosannainc.com

SPRINKLES & DECORATIONS
Bake It Pretty: bakeitpretty.com
Layer Cake Shop: layercakeshop.com
Sweet! Baking Supply: sweetbakingsupply.com
Sweet Wise: sweetwise.com

BAKING & PARTY ACCESSORIES
Aimee Broussard: aimeebroussard.com
Pine Cone Hill: pineconehill.com
Plates & Napkins: platesandnapkins.com
Shop Sweet Lulu: shopsweetlulu.com
Sucre Shop: sucreshop.com
The TomKat Studio: shoptomkat.com

ONLINE BAKING RESOURCES
Rose Cake Tutorial: iambaker.net
Frosting Cookies: Sweetopia.net, bakeat350.blogspot.
    com, sweetsugarbelle.com, thedecoratedcookie.com
General Baking: glorioustreats.com, bakerella.com,
    sweetapolita.com, bakersroyale.com

*VISIT PIZZAZZERIE.COM FOR PARTY
IDEAS & MORE SWEET RECIPES!*

First Edition
17 16 15 14   5 4 3

Text © 2013 Courtney Dial Whitmore
Photographs © 2013 Kyle Dreier

Published by
Gibbs Smith
P.O. Box 667
Layton, Utah 84041

1.800.835.4993 orders
www.gibbs-smith.com

Designed by Sugar
Printed and bound in China

Gibbs Smith books are printed on either recycled, 100% post-
consumer waste, FSC-certified papers or on paper produced
from sustainable PEFC-certified forest/controlled wood
source. Learn more at www.pefc.org.

Library of Congress Cataloging-in-Publication Data

Whitmore, Courtney Dial.
  Frostings / Courtney Dial Whitmore ; photographs by
Kyle Dreier. — First edition.
      pages cm
  ISBN 978-1-4236-3195-8
1. Icings, Cake. I. Title.
TX771.W454 2013
641.86'539—dc23
                                    2012050559

METRIC CONVERSION CHART

Volume Measurements		Weight Measurements		Temperature Conversion	
U.S.	Metric	U.S.	Metric	Fahrenheit	Celsius
1 teaspoon	5 ml	$\frac{1}{2}$ ounce	15 g	250	120
1 tablespoon	15 ml	1 ounce	30 g	300	150
$\frac{1}{4}$ cup	60 ml	3 ounces	90 g	325	160
$\frac{1}{3}$ cup	75 ml	4 ounces	115 g	350	180
$\frac{1}{2}$ cup	125 ml	8 ounces	225 g	375	190
$\frac{2}{3}$ cup	150 ml	12 ounces	350 g	400	200
$\frac{3}{4}$ cup	175 ml	1 pound	450 g	425	220
1 cup	250 ml	$2\frac{1}{4}$ pounds	1 kg	450	230